LA'S
DUI DEFENSE GUIDE

Here's What You Need To Know If Pulled Over
On Suspicion Of Drunk Driving

Ronald D. Hedding, Esq.

Speakeasy Publishing
73-03 Bell Blvd, #10
Oakland Gardens, NY 11364
www.speakeasypublishinginc.com

Ordering Information:

Quantity sales. Special discounts are available on quantity purchases by corporations, associations, and others. For details, contact the publisher at the address above.

Orders by U.S. trade bookstores and wholesalers. Please contact Speakeasy Publishing: Tel: (888) 991-2766 or visit www.speakeasypublishinginc.com.

Printed in the United States of America.

Published in 2018.

ISBN: 978-1-946481-46-7

FOREWORD

If you are reading this book, you probably received a DUI and you're trying to figure out what your next move is. DUIs can be very scary in Los Angeles and that's why I wrote this book and that's why I fight zealously for my clients. A lot of my clients are just average people who have a good job and a family and are scared to death of the legal system.

My job is to get you out of the legal system as fast as possible, to get you some control back of your life and to make sure that we protect your reputation, your record and your freedom from some of the bad things that can happen associated with a DUI case. Really, what I'm trying to do is help you get back to a normal life, to be able to drive your car without worrying about the ramifications of your DUI case. Also, because both the DMV and the court are involved, you want somebody who is an advocate and knows these entities very well and can get you the best possible outcome without you having to suffer some of the severe consequences the criminal justice system has to offer.

Finally, I am looking to get this taken care of discretely for you and as painlessly as possible so that you don't have a horrible experience with our justice system. If you've got a DUI, you probably made a mistake - it's probably something that's never going to happen again, and you need somebody who is going to do damage control and get you the result that you deserve and get you out of the system as fast as possible.

Dedication

This book is dedicated to those people who find themselves in the criminal justice system and want to get out as fast as humanly possible. It is a very scary feeling when the police place the handcuffs on you, put you in the back of the police car and take you off to jail. Being in jail, most people realize this is no place for them and they never want to go back again. My job, being a DUI defense attorney for the past twenty-five years, is to do everything humanly possible to get your matter resolved in the best possible way. I've dedicated myself to practicing DUI defense for a quarter of a century and I make it my mission to get my clients out of the system and get them back on the road as unscathed as humanly possible. We're going to sit down. We're going to decide whether your case is one that should be fought or negotiated, and then we're going to execute a plan that gets your matter taken care of professionally, discretely and to a successful outcome!

Disclaimer

This publication is intended to be used for educational purposes only. No legal advice is being given, and no attorney-client relationship is intended to be created by reading this material. The author assumes no liability for any errors or omissions or for how this book or its contents are used or interpreted or for any consequences resulting directly or indirectly from the use of this book. For legal or any other advice, please consult an experienced attorney or the appropriate expert who is aware of the specific facts of your case and is knowledgeable of the law in your jurisdiction.

Hedding Law Firm

Los Angeles Criminal Defenders

(866) 986-2092

www.la-criminaldefense.com

TESTIMONIALS

"I had a recent DUI case and retained The Hedding Law Firm. As you can imagine, I was fairly stressed out during this time and Ron (Jr. & Sr.) gave me a sense of comfort that they'd do what they could to get the best outcome. Very knowledgeable and trustworthy. I met with several lawyers in the area around the Van Nuys court and not only did I feel the most confidence in these guys but everyone at the firm are super nice people. (hard to find right?) They were able to get my .088 BAC settled to a speed contest. Thank You!!"

- Bill

****

"Hats off to both Ron Hedding Sr. and Jr. for their hard work, compassion, and tenacious spirit in fighting for the desired result in my recent DUI case. They always kept me informed and gave me reasonable expectations for the result of this case. With so much hanging on the line, and with the clear cut need to get the DUI charge against me reduced to a lesser offense, I depended on them to do all they could on my behalf. They certainly did not disappoint. I would recommend their services to friends, family, and strangers alike. If you are ever in a sticky situation that requires top notch legal services, they should undoubtedly be your first call."

- A Satisfied Client

****

"Took a very stressful situation DUI with impact and I received a minimum sentence I feel without Ron SR and Ron JR it would have been a lot worse. These guys are reasonably priced and walk you through the process very good"

- Robert

****

"I was recommended to Ron through my friend who had help from Ron for his own DUI case. I can definitely say that it was a good decision and I still thank my friend greatly for the recommendation. I never thought that I would get a DUI just a few months after my friend did, but I did. Ron helped me out so much and really made the situation and case seem better. He was very helpful and very experienced with these cases."

- A Satisfied Client

****

"Got my DUI charge dropped, was not on my record and charges also dropped for a breathalyzer refusal- Apparently this is a huge deal (to refuse the test) and comes with many consequences but Ron took care of me, and argued to preserve my rights- aside from civil and court fees- we won!"

- A Satisfied Client

****

"I was in real need of a good lawyer for my DUI case. When found Ron the first time, I was very confident of his honesty and knowledge. He did remarkable presentation in the court. He delivers above and beyond. I also would like to thank to Ron Sr. as well. Hedding Law Firm is the best and you can trust. I would highly recommend Ron Hedding. The best choice ever made."

- Lajos

****

"Hedding and his associates are very knowledgeable in regards to DUI defense cases. I was very nervous about my case, but Hedding made me feel confident and at ease during the process. He is different from other lawyers. I automatically felt that I could trust him when I went in for my initial consultation. My case was settled in no time."

- Miguel

****

"I was pulled over for a DUI in November '13. I waited up until the day before my court date to get representation from the Hedding Law Firm. Not only did he accept to represent me, he did it without taking full payment on the quoted price. (He let me pay the remainder of the balance a few weeks later) For it being my first run in with the law and my first experience hiring a lawyer, I was a little nervous about the whole thing, given all the horror stories about terrible lawyers. I never thought I would be so at ease about the whole process. I was always informed what was going on either via mail or phone call. At no point did I feel Mr. Hedding was lying or telling me what I wanted to hear. He was honest and straight to the point. I couldn't be happier with the whole experience. Oh and did I forget to mention that he got my DUI arrest down to an exhibition of speed ticket!!!!"

- A Satisfied Client

****

"I usually do not like to write reviews, but I absolutely want to do this for Ronald Hedding. Ronald is the most talented Criminal Attorney in Los Angeles. One of my friends recently had a DUI and asked me if I knew anyone. I asked my attorney friends and Ronald's name came up. I referred my friend over. He took care of everything even got my friend's case dismissed. Highly recommended. I would give 100 stars if I could."

- Anna K.

****

Table of Contents

Personal Introduction

Ronald D. Hedding is the founding member of the Hedding Law Firm. He has an extensive, well-rounded legal background in the area of criminal law. He has worked for the district attorney's office, a superior court judge, and as the guiding force behind the Hedding Law Firm. His multi-faceted experience sets him apart and puts him in an elite group of the best criminal defense attorneys in Southern California.

After establishing the Hedding Law Firm, Mr. Hedding dedicated himself towards the pursuit of zealously defending his clients to the highest professional standards. He has traveled all over this nation defending his clients and protecting their interests, reputations and freedoms. It is rare to find a criminal defense attorney with the dual ability to successfully fight a case in our jury system and the uncanny skills to negotiate a favorable disposition for his clients. It is even rarer to find an attorney with the wisdom to know the appropriate decision to make at the right time.

Mr. Hedding has been lead counsel in some of the most sensational criminal cases to be played out in Los Angeles County courthouses and at the federal level. He has received acclaim in newspapers, on the radio and in national publications. The key to Mr. Hedding's success- whether the case involves a DUI or murder charge- lies in his understanding of the US Criminal Justice System and the client's need to be informed of their best legal options so they can make the most informed decision in protecting their rights.

Current Employment Position(S)

- Managing Attorney

Bar Admissions

- U.S. Court of Appeals, 9th Circuit

- U.S. District Court Central District of California
- Superior Court for Los Angeles County
- U.S. Supreme Court

Honors and Awards

- Criminal Defense Attorney of the Year, The Editorial Staff of Consumer Business Review, 1999 – Present
- Accepted as Life Member of the National Registry of Who's Who, 2000 – Present
- Outstanding Professional Award for Dedicated Achievements in the Field of Criminal Law – ABI – USA, 2002 – Present
- Criminal Defense Attorney of the Year – The Editorial Staff of Consumer Business Review, 2003 – Present

Professional Associations and Memberships

- San Fernando Valley Bar Association, 1994 – Present
- America Bar Association, 1995 – Present
- Association of Trial Lawyers of America, 1998 – Present
- National Association of Criminal Defense Attorneys, 1999 – Present
- California Attorneys for Criminal Justice, 1995 – Present

Experience, Credentials, and Skills

- I have been named criminal defense attorney of the year in Los Angeles.
- I have won jury trials in all of the major courthouses in Los Angeles.
- My Los Angeles-based law firm is recognized by the Bar Register of Preeminent Lawyers as one of the top 5% of criminal defense law firms in Los Angeles County.
- I have been recognized in Los Angeles magazine as part of the Super Lawyers edition.
- I have won jury trials in Downtown Los Angeles federal courthouses.
- Top 5% of attorneys in California by Martendale Hubbel for ethics and legal ability.
- I have volunteered time working for the State Bar of California as a judicial nomination commissioner. I was responsible for investigating potential judges as part of a 38-person commission. I represented Los Angeles County in the process of selecting judges for the State of California.

- The president of the United States granted a presidential pardon for one of my Los Angeles-based clients.
- I have been involved in a published legal opinion related to a case that I have handled in one of the Los Angeles courts.
- As a Los Angeles defense attorney, I have written articles on criminal defense subject matters in local bar publications.
- AVVO has rated me Superb 10 out of 10 for skill and legal abilities in the Los Angeles courts.

CHAPTER 1
UNDER THE INFLUENCE

In California, the simple definition of being under the influence is being unable to drive a vehicle as a sober person would under similar circumstance. When someone is evaluating whether or not someone is under the influence for the purposes of a DUI, they're not necessarily evaluating whether that person is drunk. A lot of people don't realize that you don't have to be drunk in order to get a DUI; you just have to be under the influence to the point of being unable to safely operate a motor vehicle.

This is why there will be two charges against a defendant. One of those charges is 23152A, which says that you have alcohol in your system and cannot safely operate a motor vehicle. This charge has nothing to do with your blood alcohol content; you could be below 0.08 in California and still get convicted for a DUI. The other section is 23152B, which says that if you have a blood alcohol level of 0.08 or greater, then you are presumed to be unable to safely operate a motor vehicle. That is a presumption that must be rebutted in order to avoid a conviction for DUI.

In order for the police to be able to say that a person was driving for the purposes of a DUI, the car typically has to have been moving. However, a lot of times people call me and say, "Listen, the police came and I wasn't driving when they got there." So, then the question becomes based on the surrounding circumstances. Can the police prove that the person was driving at some point, and if so, when? The police would have to get the blood or breath test results and be able to extrapolate backwards to figure out what the BAC was at the time of driving. One way of doing this would be to find a witness who reports seeing the person driving at a certain time. However, the police will usually just ask the person whether or not they drove the car, what time they were driving and when they were drinking.

It's very common for the police to find a person who is sitting or sleeping in their car and try to charge them with DUI by determining when they were driving. If the car was found to be blocking the road, then according to the case law in Los Angeles, that would be considered driving. If the car was legally parked, not moving, and the keys were in the ignition, then the person in that car would not necessarily be considered to be driving. In fact, I've won a number of cases under those circumstances.

Definition Of DUI In California State Law

In California, the legislature has determined that you can be charged with a DUI if you drive with an alcohol content of 0.08 or greater. The other way to be charged with a DUI is if you have alcohol in your system and you cannot safely operate a motor vehicle. Whether or not you can safely operate a motor vehicle is determined by whether or not you can pass a field sobriety test that the police administer. It's also determined by how you were driving, walking and speaking.

Implied Consent Law In DUI Cases

Since driving in California is considered a privilege and not a right, there is an implied consent law which you agree to when you receive your California driver's license. Specifically, you agree to consent to a blood or breath test if the police ever suspect you to be under the influence of drugs or alcohol and determine that you cannot safely operate a motor vehicle. If you refuse to consent, then you will be held as a DUI refusal and will lose your driving privileges for one year. In addition, it will be automatically presumed that you are DUI.

Chapter 2
Pulled Over On Suspicion Of DUI?

If you've been pulled over on suspicion of DUI in Los Angeles County, the police will start asking you questions in order to determine whether or not you are intoxicated or unable to drive safely. They will smell your breath to see if they smell alcohol, but they will also directly ask you whether or not you have been drinking. Most people will tell the police that they have had a couple of drinks. At that point, the officer will tell you to exit your vehicle and they will begin conducting the field sobriety tests.

If the officer has a preliminary alcohol screening device (PAS), then they are probably going to have you blow into that because they don't want to waste a trip to the police station. If they ultimately determine that you are unable to safely operate a motor vehicle because of your alcohol content, then they are going to arrest you and take you to do a breath or blood test.

What Are Officers Looking For During Roadside Field Sobriety Tests?

The officers are going to be looking for signs of intoxication. They are going to see if you can follow their instructions and they will check your pupils for dilation or bouncing. They will usually have you walk in a line, and then take nine steps forward and nine steps back. They are going to have you tilt your head back and touch your nose, and they may also ask you to recite the alphabet backwards. During all of these tests, they are going to be evaluating you for signs of intoxication. As you can see, this is a very subjective evaluation and sometimes the police are not perfectly accurate.

Am I Required To Perform Standardized Field Sobriety Tests?

You are not required to submit to the preliminary alcohol screening test or the field sobriety tests. If the police determine that you may be intoxicated and cannot safely operate a motor vehicle, then you are going to have to submit to a blood or breath test. If you refuse, then you can lose your license for one year and there will be a presumption that you cannot safely operate a motor vehicle. So, it's a bad move to refuse the blood or breath test.

What Happens Once I'm Arrested And Taken To Jail In Los Angeles County? Can I Bond Out?

Once you have been taken to jail, you can bond out if they put a bail on the case. However, if you did not get in an accident or hurt anyone, then you probably ought to just wait until the police test you and cite you out. They will usually cite you out once they determine that you are safe to go back out on the street.

Their biggest concern is that they will let you out while you are still intoxicated and that you will end up behind the wheel again. If that happened and you were to injure or kill someone, then they would be held responsible for that. So, even if you bond out, the police are probably going to make you wait to ensure that the alcohol has left your system. In fact, they often have defendants perform additional breath tests before allowing them to leave the station. If you have been charged with felony DUI, then you may end up having to bail out.

Locating A Friend Or Family Member After A DUI Arrest

If you can identify the location of the police department responsible for the arrest, then you will be able to determine where your family member or friend is being held. For example, if they were arrested in West San Fernando Valley, then you will know that they are being held at the police department in that area of the San Fernando Valley. Attorneys and bail bondsmen can quickly obtain information regarding the whereabouts of a person who has been arrested. If you let enough time pass, the person will be put in the sheriff's system and you'll be able to see when they're going to go to court. The quickest and most efficient way to find out is to call an attorney.

CHAPTER 3
DO I HAVE TO TAKE BREATHALYZER TEST?

Yes, you will have to take the breathalyzer test at the station in LA County. However, you can also choose a blood test, in which case they would take you to a hospital or to a police station that is equipped to administer a blood test.

What Happens To My Driver's License If I Refuse Breath Test At Police Station?

If it's determined that you are a refusal in LA County, you are going to lose your driver's license for one year and you will not be able to get a restricted license for that one-year period. That's a horrible outcome, because even if you had consented to the test and were over 0.08, you would have been able to get your license back within 30 days. So, it's very costly to refuse these tests due to the one-year driver's license suspension.

What Paperwork Will I Leave The Jail With After I Have Bonded Out Of Jail On A DUI Charge?

When the police let you go in Los Angeles County, they will typically give you a citation that lists the time and location of your court date. If you cannot find this information on your citation, an attorney should be able to help you do so.

If you are forced to post a bail, then the bail bond company will give you a half-slip that will list the time and location of your court date. If you are not given that paperwork (which occasionally does happen), then you should contact the arresting agency or an attorney.

Why Are The Days Following A DUI Arrest Critical For My Driver's License In Los Angeles County?

When you get arrested for a DUI, you will be given a temporary driver's license that states in both English and

Spanish that you have 10 days to contact the DMV. If you do not contact the DMV within those 10 days, then your license will be automatically suspended. It may be helpful to seek the assistance of an attorney who can deal with the DMV and set up the hearing for you, and ask for a stay on any suspension until you get the hearing. It's crucial that you take these steps within 10 days of having received your temporary license. After 30 days, your temporary license will expire and your suspension will begin.

How Often Should I Expect To Meet With My DUI Attorney To Discuss The Case In The First Month After An Arrest?

The initial meeting is crucial because that's when you give your attorney all of the information that you have and discuss how you want your case handled. After the first meeting, you can meet with your attorney as many times as you want or as often as you and your attorney deem appropriate. You want to ensure that you understand everything that is going on and that you have the best strategy together.

The second meeting with your attorney is the most important because that is when the attorney will have all of the paperwork (police reports, test results etc.) related to your case. Once all of that information has been collected, you can have a meaningful conversation with your attorney regarding what the prosecution has against you and whether you want to fight or negotiate the case.

CHAPTER 4

FINDING A QUALIFIED ATTORNEY

There are a number of different ways to find a qualified attorney to represent you or a loved one in a DUI case. If you have come to this website or you're reading this book, then you have already found one who has been handling DUI cases for 25 years. You definitely want to obtain an attorney right away so that you or your loved one's rights can be preserved and so that the best possible outcome can be obtained.

Can A DUI Attorney Help My Friend Or Family Member Get Out Of Jail Immediately After A DUI Arrest?

An attorney can absolutely help you or your family member get out of jail immediately after a DUI arrest by arguing to the judge for an OR release. If you are not released before your court date, then we are looking to determine whether or not you are a danger to the community or a flight risk. When making a determination regarding a bond condition or the possibility of being released on your own recognizance, the court will consider how long you have lived in Los Angeles, and whether or not you have a job, family and property. The court will also consider the nature of your conduct, what you did, how fast you were going, and how dangerously you were behaving. They just want to make sure that you are not going to cause another accident, because then they could be responsible for it. Depending on how high the blood alcohol level was, they may hold you until they can ensure that you are sober and no longer a danger to the community.

Can I Hire Someone Else If I Am Not Satisfied With The Services Provided By My DUI Attorney?

If you are not satisfied with the services provided by your DUI attorney, then you can absolutely hire a different attorney. You can simply call that attorney and tell them that you are no longer interested in having them represent you. The new attorney that you find would be able to contact the initial law firm, communicate with the DMV and take care of the criminal court case.

Chapter 5
Can I Contact An Attorney Before Taking Breath Or Blood Test?

You can certainly try to contact an attorney before deciding whether or not to take the breath or blood test, but realistically speaking, the police are not going to let you use your phone while they are investigating you for DUI. It's unlikely that you would be able to successfully discuss things with an attorney at that time. If you have been pulled over and the police believe that you have been drinking and driving, most attorneys will advise you to cooperate with them and take the breath or blood test. If you refuse, then you will lose your driver's license for one year. In addition, you will probably end up with a DUI conviction because it will be hard to rebut the presumption related to a DUI refusal in Los Angeles County.

How Do I Know What To Do After I Am Released from Jail?

If you get cited out of jail, then you'll probably get a ticket that lists the date, time and location of your next court date. If you get bailed out, the bail bond company will typically give you a half slip of paper that will list your court date and what you were booked for. You will want to take that paperwork to a qualified DUI defense attorney who can help you out. The paperwork should also list an ECI reading, which is the reading from the breath test.

Can I Still Drive After Being Arrested For DUI?

If you have a California driver's license and you are arrested in LA County for a DUI, the police will usually take that license from you and send it to the DMV. They will give you a pink slip that will serve as a temporary license for 30 days. If you were to be pulled over during the 30-day period after the arrest, then you could show the police that pink slip as proof that you are driving lawfully. Once you hire an attorney, they will call the DMV and set up a DMV hearing. If the DMV hearing is set beyond that 30-day time period, then you will get another temporary license that will allow you drive up until the DMV hearing date.

Mistakes To Avoid After Or During A DUI Arrest

It's important to avoid making the mistake of giving the police information, because they will only try to use it against you in a later prosecution. This will make it more difficult for your attorney to represent you. Another mistake would be to attempt to handle a DUI case without an attorney. Since you are not an attorney, you won't know which questions to ask or how to properly defend your case.

Will I Have To Go To Court In The First Month Following A DUI Arrest?

In Los Angeles County, you will typically have a court date within about 30 days of a DUI arrest. If you do not appear at that court date, there will be a warrant issued for your arrest. However, if you hire an attorney, that attorney may be able to make that first court appearance for you. That is the practice of my firm; we attend the first court appearance, review the paperwork, and speak to the prosecutor in order to get a feel for what we are up against. We will ask for two or three weeks in order to continue reviewing all of the paperwork, allow you to review it and decide how to proceed.

CHAPTER 6
THE FIRST 24 HOURS AFTER A DUI ARREST

Once the police have arrested you, they have made a determination that you failed the field sobriety tests or that you're just too intoxicated to take the field sobriety tests. They are going to put the handcuffs on you, place you in the back of the police car and then ask whether or not you want to take a blood or a breath test. You should realize that driving in Los Angeles and throughout California is a privilege and not a right. As a result, if the police believe in their subjective mind that you're too intoxicated to safely operate a motor vehicle, then you will have to take one of those tests. If you don't, it'll be counted as a refusal and it will automatically be assumed that you're guilty of DUI. That is a presumption that's very difficult to rebut. They will then either drive you to the hospital to take your blood or to the police station so that you can submit to the breath test.

Some of the police locations will have you take a blood and a breath test. Before having you submit to a breath test, they will observe you for 15 minutes to make sure that nothing gets in your mouth that could affect the results. They are ensuring that you do not burp, vomit, or do anything else that could affect the results. Then they will have you blow into the machine twice in order to obtain two readings. At that point, and depending on what your reading is, they will keep you in custody until they deem that you are safe to be let go. Sometimes people will be let go within an hour or two, especially if they are cooperative. Other people may be kept for several hours.

If you refuse to take either test, then you can probably expect to be kept for many hours. Once they let you go, they're going to give you a citation slip with the date on which you are to appear in court. That date is usually about 30 days after the initial arrest. If your BAC is very high or if you are charged with a felony, then they're going to put a bail on you. At that point, you would have to post a bail in order to be released, and you should consider hiring a DUI defense attorney.

What Rights Do I Have If I Am Arrested In Los Angeles County On DUI Charges?

Once you are arrested, you have the right to remain silent. You do not have to give any incriminating statements. You just need to make sure that you are being cooperative and that you submit to a blood or breath test. If you don't, they will write that you refused and there will be a presumption that will be difficult to rebut. If people had the option of refusing the tests without any consequences, then anyone would be able to get away with DUI. However, you do have the right not to take those field sobriety tests. If you are not drunk, then you should probably just cooperate with them, because if you blow a value of 0.05 or lower, then they will probably just let you go.

Will I Be Arraigned Before I Am Released From Jail After A DUI Charge?

Whether or not you will be arraigned before being released from jail will depend. If they put a bail on you, then you should be arraigned within a couple of business days of being arrested. You'll be able to talk to your attorney and then you'll enter a not guilty, guilty, or a no contest plea. After you are arraigned, the judge will set the bail. If you don't bail out, then you will remain in custody until the next court date. On a first or second-time DUI, bail is not usually set. Instead, they'll just release you on your own recognizance.

At What Point Can I Contact An Attorney After Being Arrested For DUI?

You should contact an attorney as soon as you can. An attorney can guide you through the process and advise you on what to do and what not to do. Various things can happen during an arrest. Sometimes people don't get all of the paperwork or information that they need, and they will be unsure of what their next steps should be. You should definitely contact an attorney who has successfully handled cases in the court where your case is going to be pending. You want an attorney who has the qualifications necessary to successfully guide you through the DUI process in LA.

CHAPTER 7

MEETING WITH MY ATTORNEY IN THE FIRST FEW DAYS AFTER A DUI

You will want to meet with your attorney within the first few days of having been arrested for DUI so that you can give them all of the information related to the arrest. You should be honest with your attorney about what happened; don't put a spin on things. You should tell your attorney how you think the prosecutor and the police will tell their version of events, and you should not omit anything. The attorney will then ask you to tell your version of events so that they will be prepared to represent you in the best possible way.

Will I Have To Meet With A Pre-Trial Probation Officer In The First Month Following a DUI Arrest?

If you are being charged with a misdemeanor DUI in Los Angeles, then you probably won't be put on formal probation or have to deal with a probation officer. If you are put on summary probation for a case, then you cannot violate the terms of that probation or incur new charges. If you end up being convicted for a felony DUI, then you will most likely be put on probation, but that would not occur within the first 30 days of the arrest. Instead, that would probably occur later down the road, and your attorney would explain how to interact with the probation department.

Can Pre-Trial Counseling Help My DUI Case?

Before getting involved with any counseling or AA meetings, you are going to want to sit down with an attorney. Some attorneys will recommend that their clients take certain actions without knowing anything about their case. It's not a cookie-cutter situation; we don't just do the same thing in every DUI case in Los Angeles County.

If your blood alcohol level was very high and you were behaving dangerously, then they might think that you have a problem with alcohol and it may be a good idea to take some AA classes in coordination with your attorney. Alternatively, you may want to enter an inpatient or outpatient program.

If you don't have an alcohol problem and you just made a mistake, then you don't necessarily want to start going to AA meetings. If you do, the prosecutors may assume that you have a problem with alcohol, and as a result, they may add punishments. So, let your attorney be your guide. Give them all of the necessary information and they will properly advise you on how to proceed.

The Best Advice For Prospective Clients

In the days and weeks that follow a DUI arrest in Los Angeles County, my clients and I will have a meeting of the minds in order to discuss what exactly happened and how we are going to deal with it. I let my clients know how they can help me and what to expect. I find that knowing what they are up against helps give clients peace of mind. We figure out what our goal is and determine how we can go about getting the best resolution.

Once I have the answer to that question, we put the wheels in motion and start doing things that can help us. For example, I might suggest that the client enter some sort of program or collect character letters from friends and family in order to demonstrate that they are a good person. There are a number of things that can be done, but the specifics of what those are will depend on the circumstances of the case at hand.

CHAPTER 8
PULLED OVER ON SUSPICION OF USING DRUGS?

Before someone is pulled over on suspicion of using drugs, the officer will evaluate their driving. If the officer sees that they are driving in a manner that would indicate being under the influence of something, then they will pull that person over, approach them, and evaluate how they're speaking and what their eyes look like. The police are specifically trained to identify people who are under the influence of prescription medication or a drug that would affect their ability to safely operate a motor vehicle. A lot of times, they'll just directly ask a driver whether or not they've had any alcohol or used any drugs. This would be their first line of attack.

Next, the police would call out an expert who is trained to identify whether someone is under the influence of some sort of narcotic that would hinder their ability to drive a motor vehicle. Finally, they would request that the person take a urine test so they could analyze through a toxicological screen whether or not that particular individual was under the influence of any substances.

Do Police Request Field Sobriety Tests In Drug DUI Cases?

If an officer suspects that a person is under the influence of drugs and requests that they perform field sobriety tests, then they are probably inexperienced. This is because the field sobriety tests are meant to identify whether someone is under the influence of alcohol rather than some type of prescription or narcotic. If an officer does use the standard field sobriety tests, then their credibility can be attacked by a good criminal defense/ DUI defense attorney. More experienced officers would have a drug recognition expert come out to the scene if they suspect a person to be under the influence of prescription drugs or narcotics.

Test For Drugs In A Person's System

Oftentimes the police are unable to determine whether or not someone is under the influence of a drug, alcohol, or both. So, first they'll have the suspect take the handheld breath test to test for alcohol. If that registers zero but the officer still suspects that the person is under the influence of something, then they'll ask that person to take a blood test and/or a urine test. Both blood and urine tests are able to identify whether someone has a narcotic in their system that would deem them unable to safely operate a motor vehicle.

Metabolites Or Active Compounds Test In A Marijuana Related DUI Case

Before testing for metabolites or active compounds in a marijuana related case, the police will first walk up to the vehicle and say they smell marijuana. Then they will look at the person and see how they are acting and try to determine whether or not the person seems impacted by the use of marijuana and/or able to operate a motor vehicle. Then they will usually do a urine test to determine whether or not the person is under the influence of marijuana.

Many years ago, the police could only determine whether or not someone had THC in their system. Now the tests are more sophisticated and can actually determine the level of marijuana intoxication. This obviously helps the prosecutors determine whether or not the person could safely operate a motor vehicle.

Drug Recognition Expert

A drug recognition expert is a person who has been specifically trained to identify whether or not a person is under the influence of a particular narcotic or drug. A lot of people think that only illegal narcotics are illegal to use while driving, but the truth is that any substance which could impact your ability to safely operate a motor vehicle can cause you to receive a DUI.

Oftentimes, people are taking prescription medications that are prescribed by their doctors and that's causing them to become involved in an accident or not be able to safely operate a motor vehicle. The drug recognition experts use certain tests to determine whether or not a person can safely operate a motor vehicle. They also test to determine the type and quantity of a substance in someone's system.

CHAPTER 9
REFUSING A DRUG TEST

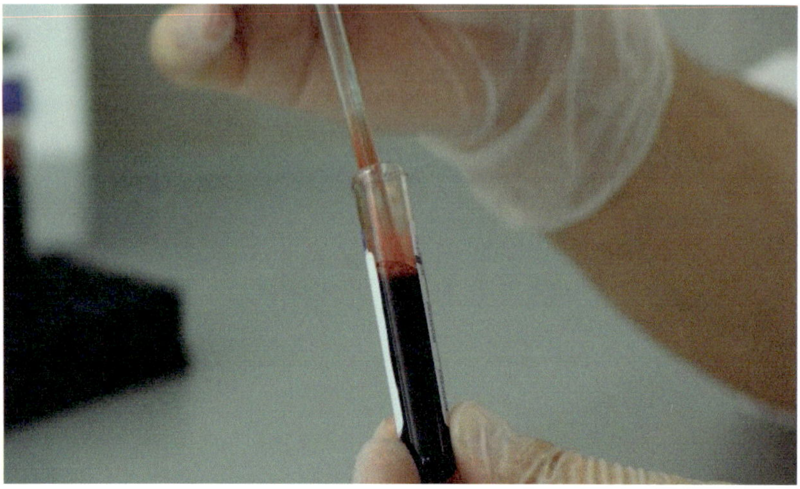

Yes, someone can refuse a drug test in a DUI investigation. The police can attempt to get a warrant for a blood test, but that is not likely to happen because it would take too long. If there is an accident involved in a DUI, then the police will do a forced a blood draw, whereby they hold the person down and obtain a sample of blood. This is usually only something they will do when there is an accident; they would never do this on a regular stop.

If there is no alcohol in your system and the police suspect that you're under the influence of some sort of drug, then they can demand that you take a blood test or urine test. If you refuse, then they can count it as a refusal and you will lose your driver's license for one year. This is all true under the assumption that the police did everything they were supposed to regarding the refusal law and letting you know that if you don't take the blood test or the urine test, then you will lose your driver's license for one year.

How Reliable Are Blood Tests?

The blood test is usually more reliable than the breath test. Oftentimes it is hard to determine when a person actually took a medication or narcotic based on a blood sample. However, the blood test usually helps the prosecutors prove their case simply because it will show that there were drugs in a person's system. Sometimes people mix alcohol with drugs or narcotics. If someone's blood tests positive for a substance which could impair their ability to safely operate a motor vehicle, then that is a weapon that could be used to prove that the person was DUI. On the other hand, if a person does not have narcotics in their system and they didn't take anything that could impact their ability to drive safely, then the blood will be their best friend. It will prove innocence.

Should I Admit To Taking Prescription Or Illegal Drugs In Front Of Law Enforcement?

A lot of people try to indicate that they've taken some sort of cold medicine or that they're on some sort of prescription medication, thinking that saying so will help them talk their way out of a DUI. The bottom line is that if you take anything that affects your ability to safely operate a motor vehicle, then the police can arrest you for a DUI. The fact that a medication is prescribed to you is not an excuse. So, usually your best bet is not to admit anything to the police. As part of your privilege to drive, you must cooperate with the police if they ask you to take a blood or breath test. However, you certainly don't have to voluntarily answer all of their questions, especially those which might incriminate you. You can tell the police that if they are going to ask you specific questions and try to incriminate you, then you're going to need to speak to your lawyer.

Drug DUI Cases And Alcohol DUI Cases

The level of difficulty between defending a drug DUI case and an alcohol DUI case is probably about the same. In a drug DUI case, the first question will be to determine whether or not there is any sort of a narcotic or prescription medication in your system. In an alcohol DUI case, the first question will be to determine whether or not there is any alcohol in your system. In either case, the mere presence of a substance in your system does not necessarily mean that you are unable to safely operate a motor vehicle for the purposes of a DUI.

The same evaluation is used for both alcohol related DUIs and drug related DUIs. The police will consider the reason for the stop, how you were driving, how you are speaking and whether or not your eyes appear watery or bloodshot. If they get a chance to see you walk, then they are going to evaluate your gait. In other words, are you staggering or can you walk around easily? So, the same evaluation is used in both scenarios.

CHAPTER 10
PENALTIES IN DUI CASES

There is a whole array of penalties associated with DUIs. For a first offense, a person is generally looking at a minimum by the legislature of $390, plus a 200% penalty assessment up to a maximum of $1,000. They're typically going to be put on three to five years of summary probation where they don't have to report to a probation officer. They're also going to be required to participate in an alcohol program. In LA County, there are a number of different alcohol programs, including a three-month, six-month, nine-month, 18-month and 30-month program. For a first offense DUI, a person is usually looking at a three-month alcohol program. These are the standard bare-minimum penalties that a person would be looking at.

Depending on how severe or serious a DUI was, other penalties may result, including community service, community labor and jail time. In the most severe cases, a person could be forced to do the hospital morgue program or attend a one-day Mothers Against Drunk Driving seminar. A person could also be forced to wear a scram bracelet on their ankle that detects alcohol and ordered not to drink any alcohol during the probationary period. There are a slew of different things that prosecutors and judges have at their disposal in these cases.

Installation Of Ignition Interlock Device

An ignition interlock device is usually ordered when a person seeks a restricted driver's license after having had their full driving privileges suspended. Since a person's driving privileges are usually only suspended in alcohol related DUI cases, people are usually not required to get an ignition interlock device when they receive a drug related DUI.

Role Of Science In Defense Strategies In Drug DUI Cases

If the case is fought at the jury trial level, science will play a role because each side would call an expert to discuss whether or not the particular defendant appeared to be intoxicated to a level that they could not safely operate a motor vehicle. Obviously, the defense would want to find an expert who would say, "No, that person was not unable to safely operate a motor vehicle based on what was found in their system, based on what was indicated by the police when they saw them driving and based on what was indicated by the police when they later arrested them and had them do a field sobriety or drug recognition test."

The prosecutor's expert would try to argue the opposite and claim that some of the factors that are pointed out in the police report do indicate that the person was intoxicated to the level that they could not safely operate a motor vehicle. Ultimately, a jury would decide, based on the facts of the case, whether or not the person was innocent or guilty of the DUI in Los Angeles.

Why Is It Critical To Hire An Experienced Attorney?

The bottom-line is that there is no cookie-cutter solution to DUI defenses, especially those involving narcotics or prescription medications; each case depends on its own facts. Having an attorney who's been down the road that you're about to travel is crucial in making sure that every single possible defense is asserted on your behalf. You want to be given the opportunity to attempt to prove your innocence. If you are guilty, then your attorney is going to do damage control and make sure that you receive the lowest possible charge and the lowest possible penalties related to your DUI.

CHAPTER 11
IMPACT OF A PRIOR DUI ARREST ON A DUI CASE

If you have a prior DUI conviction within 10 years of a new case, then your new DUI will be treated as a second offense. The penalties will be much more severe on a second offense. You will be looking at mandatory jail time, 18 months in an alcohol program (instead of three months), as well as a higher fine and punishment in criminal court. It behooves you to hire a DUI defense attorney who is local to your courthouse so that you can come up with a strategy for handling your second DUI.

Factors That Would Enhance Or Aggravate A DUI Charge In LA County

There are absolutely factors that can aggravate a DUI charge in Los Angeles County. In fact, the prosecutors look for aggravating factors when determining how they are going to handle your case and how harsh they and the judge will be on you. Some of the factors that they will consider include how fast you were driving, in what manner you were driving, whether or not you were involved in an accident, whether or not there were any injuries, and how you dealt with the police. If you were cooperative with the police and were stopped for something minor, such as failing to turn on your turn signal, then your attorney is going to be in a much stronger position to mitigate your case to a lesser charge.

Sentences For First Time And Multiple DUI Convictions In LA County

There are many different sentences that can be doled out depending on what exactly happened. On a typical DUI, you will be looking at doing a three, six, nine, 18 or 30 month-long alcohol program, which will be negotiated by your defense attorney. You are also going to pay a minimum fine of $390, as well as a 200% penalty assessment up to a maximum fine of $1000. Additionally, you will be looking at serving a probationary period of three to five years, depending on how serious the case is.

Other punishments include community service, community labor and participating in the hospital morgue program. As a participant in the hospital morgue program, you have to write a letter to the judge after you visit the morgue and see what happens to people who drink and drive. You would also have to do a VIP program, which is a one-day seminar put on by Mothers Against Drunk Driving. You can be required to attend AA or NA meetings, especially when you are out on your own recognizance. Depending on your danger level, there are a number of other restrictions they can put on you. For example, they can make you wear a SCRAM bracelet, which determines whether or not you've had any alcohol.

You are definitely not going to be able to drive during the probationary period with any alcohol on your person or in your system. They can even disallow you from consuming any alcohol during your probationary period. It's very important to get an attorney who has been down this road before, who knows how to handle these cases and who will do everything they can to minimize the damage that a DUI can cause.

Alternative Programs Available To DUI Offenders In LA County

If somebody has a very bad alcohol or narcotics problem and they are facing a significant amount of jail time for DUI, sometimes we can get them into a live-in program instead of jail. A program of this sort can help to address the root of their problem, allow them to avoid jail time and hopefully put them in a much better position to move forward. If this is not the case, then there are bare minimums that the prosecutors and judges must abide by for a first, second, third and fourth DUI.

What Can My Firm Do To Help You With Your DUI Case In Los Angeles County?

Having handled DUIs in Los Angeles County for over 25 years, we can go over everything with you at the initial meeting. We will be getting to know your version of events and your life story. We want to be able to tell the prosecutor and the judge positive things about you, because the police typically focus only on the bad aspects of a person. We focus on damage control and take the position of "Do it once, do it right and never do it again." It's traumatizing when you get a DUI because you are arrested and essentially lose control of your life.

After our first meeting, we're going to have a game plan. You are going to know what you are up against, what you can do to help us and how exactly we are going to help you. You are going to see the light at the end of the tunnel. We are going to help you put the whole event behind you as soon as possible and in a professional, discreet manner.

What's The Next Step?

Get together a list of questions and come in for a face-to-face meeting to begin the process of seizing back control of your life and getting out of the criminal justice system as fast as possible... Make the call today (866) 986-2092.

INDEX

NOTES

Made in the USA
Monee, IL
05 November 2026

67385058R00043